Searching My Soul

Rose Marie West
2006, 2007, 2008
U.S.A. Poet Ambassador

Rose Marie West

PublishAmerica
Baltimore

© 2005 by Rose Marie West.

All rights reserved. No part of this book may be reproduced, stored in a retrieval system or transmitted in any form or by any means without the prior written permission of the publishers, except by a reviewer who may quote brief passages in a review to be printed in a newspaper, magazine or journal.

First printing

At the specific preference of the author, PublishAmerica allowed this work to remain exactly as the author intended, verbatim, without editorial input.

ISBN: 1-4241-0808-X
PUBLISHED BY PUBLISHAMERICA, LLLP
www.publishamerica.com
Baltimore

Printed in the United States of America

Dedication

I dedicate this book to the memory of my Mom and Dad.
To all my family, friends, and my boyfriend;
They all stood by me and supported me. To the school children and online people who helped and appreciated my poetry. The encouragement and support from everyone is deeply appreciated. A special dedication goes to God for the gift of life and writing that he gave me!

Acknowledgments

To my Dad that taught me about expressing myself through poetry. To Krissy for encouraging me to post my first poem online. To Gary who helped me afford to keep writing. To Geoff who got me to reflect life in my poetry and do spell check. To Billy who wouldn't let me give up and always believed in me. To everyone that promoted my poetry. To Ron Kisner for his work on this book!

Index

The Spirit of Poetry
13

Getting Closer to Year's End
14

Purity of Love
15

Why Do People Fear Death
16

Telephone Please Don't Ring
17

You Light a Candle I Light One Too
18

You Are What Makes It a Home
19

A Grandma's Love
20

In My Mind
21

My Little Puppy Named Sue
22

I Wait by the Fire Place
23

We Share Our Memories
24

Babe You Are My Valentine
26

Grants
27

Do You Know
29

Depression Pit
30

Don't Call Me a Family Friend
32

Passionate You
34

Colors and All
35

Drifting at an Ocean's Sea
36

An Angel's Gift of a Rose
37

I Long for a Love Like You
39

I Love You Just as I Have Said
40

What is Life About
41

Best of Holidays
42

God is Hearing You
43

My Web of Words
45

Mary the Fairy
47

While You Are Away
48

Grateful to Be Together Through Time
49

A Quiet Good Bye
50

This Little Angel
51

You Are What Lights Up My Life
52

Oh My Dear Mom
53

My Quiet Moment, A Blessing to Me
55

My Precious Mother
56

On This Night
57

When I Feel You
58

A Day of Wonder
59

Mommy and Daddy's Baby
60

Did You Know Son?
61

I'm a Baby to Be
62

My Amazing Grace
63

A Beloved Mother's Love
64

In a Room of Rhymes
65

A Mother's Passing Love
66

The War and Me
67

I Caught a Falling Angel
69

In Honor of My Mom and Dad
70

Mother's Wisdom
72

My Letter from Momma
73

In My Garden of Life
75

The Spirit of Poetry

Poetry is a comfort in our soul and mind,
that our spirit relates from time to time

Poetry is like the rushing of leaves,
dancing freely in the gentle breeze

Each word of poetry is like music to the ears,
like raindrops you love and long to hear

Poetry is as beautiful as the rainbows,
its colors so vivid and bright the soul glows

Poetry is a spirit of healing, I know,
for it has healed my aching soul

Poetry can bring a smile where there was a frown,
it can bring our burst of laughter abound

Poetry can bring peacefulness at times of death,
that comforts and stills the crying and lest one rest

Poetry is words to the musical song of love,
it makes a swirling of great joy, that is a gift from above

Poetry is words to express what one can not say,
words they so much want and need to convey

Poetry is the thoughts we feel day after day,
Poetry is the sound of life we share this way

The soul of life is in every way,
The spirit of poetry, we live every day!

Getting Closer to Year's End

Summer is gone and now it is fall
I think of the good and the bad and all
I think of spring and all it brings
I think of summer as the birds sing
I think of colors as leaves begin to fall
I think of winter and Christmas and all
I rejoice over good things that were well done
I mourn over wives, daughters, husband, father, and sons
as they fight for our freedom and for our rights
But I know they long to hold their loved ones tight
a reflection of who I am and how I feel
Makes me stand tall and as strong as steel
But yet as gentle, graceful, and fragile as a butterfly
when I hold a baby or a child in need as time goes by
For in my hands, their future and their lives I hold
A tear, a hope, or a dream they have, vivid and bold,
It is up to me to make a difference, good and right
In my heart, I ask God for help and hold His love for me tight
These things are things I pray about tonight
as I go to sleep, looking at the moonlight

Purity of Love

To prove the purity of my love
as pure as the heavens above
The music in my soul cries out loud
proclaiming my love strong and proud
in my nakedness there is nothing to hide
I give to you myself and my love with pride
the loyalty of love I will abide
For honor of your love here deep inside
Where my heart was once empty is now full
your love and mine have now joined in a pool
of undying love
Blessed now by God in Heaven above,
Angel's trumpets play as only they can
You and I now join hands
Proclaiming proudly our love,
Descending from heven accompanied by a dove,
As a sign of proof of
our love,
It is now blessed with God's own love,
So go forward and always share,
Your proven purity of love, sweet and rare

Why Do People Fear Death

Why do people fear death?
Why not find comfort in their rest

Because we love and miss them I guess,
and we do miss them...yes

They give life their best,
they sustained life's test

But now it is time to let them go and let them rest,
find comfort in that they shared with you their best

Death is part, of who we are inside,
like the passing of the ocean's tide

We share our lives with them...right?
Sometimes even turned their days to sunny and bright

Sometimes set up with them all night,
helping them with their problems and holding them tight

They live life with us together,
in all kinds of sunny and stormy weather

Yes they give us their best,
because they loved us too I guess

So do not fear the coming of death,
give them comfort and then let them go to rest

Find comfort and peace in their death,
by letting them go, let them go and let them be at peaceful rest

Telephone Please Don't Ring

Telephone please don't ring,
it is just bad news that you bring
A friend with open heart surgery and 6 clips
God be with him whispers from my lips
A cousin with breast cancer she fights for her life
she is such a caring and loving wife
Telephone please don't ring,
I can't bear the bad news that you bring
Yet another friend has died
With out saying my good-byes
Doctors has ordered for me more test
I am so tired from them can't they give me some rest
Oh telephone please don't ring
Let me set a while and let me sing
Let me feel a moment of happiness that it brings
Let me imagine happy bell tones of harmony that rings and rings
A man I know, his leg badly burned
The grafts not healing brings me concern
A cousin in the hospital with colon surgery,
he is tired and says he is weary,
Telephone please don't ring
I can't bear the sadness that you bring
Telephone please don't ring!

You Light a Candle
I Light One Too

When you light your candle I light one too
We pray about things we need to do
We watch a flicker of light
as it brings to us hope tonight
You read a verse and look for answers to things
I look for answers too and the happiness it will bring
You look me in the eye,
and I wonder why
Then you hold me
Then I know why, it is plain to see
because we share life together you and me
and that is how we make it through
Together we figure our what we need to do
You light a candle and I light one too,
because you know I love you too!

You Are What Makes It a Home

When the world gets unbearable to live some days,
with all its responsibilities, trials,and troubles more than one
can say
I come home to you
and your loving smile too
You surround me with the thing I love
Like my poetry and art a gift from above,
soft quieting music so peaceful and calming
soft flickering candle light
warms a smile with in me bright
You are what makes it a home to come to
so caring and loving, I am blessed to have you
You let me know you understand
and you give me all the freedom that you can,
to let my soul quiet and calm while you hold my hand
a soothing touch
Lets me know it is ok, there is no rush
and when my restless spirit is at rest
you give me what I love the very best
and you let me know you love it too
for you give me all of you
and Babe I love you too
That is what makes it a home worth coming home to!

Grandma's Love

As a Grandma lays dying in bed,
her daughter sets her with her hand upon her head
A deep silence of morning deep with in her,
for the in pending lose of her mother as it were
A unbearable sound of crying inside of her soul,
in her eyes a grieving that has left her unwhole,
when all at once her own daughter touches her with a tap
then lays her head on her mom's lap
The little girl gave her grandma a kiss on the cheek,
her Grandma's eyes open as if to peek,
at the face that kissed her with pure love,
I'll love you always even from above,
this in her dying breath I felt her love,
the heart pours of pain with the lose of grandma's love,
as she feels her soul leave and go up above,
but the Gift she leaves us is her love!

In My Mind

When I need you, and I'm feeling blue
In my mind you need me too

When I long for your touch,
in my mind I feel a flutter and a rush

When I need to share with you
in my mind I feel you

When I need to feel your kiss
in my mind, your lips are my wish,

When I need to see your eyes,
in my mind loving reflections and warm signs

When I cry,
in my mind you sigh

When in my passion I want you
in my mind you show me passion too!

But when in my mind I need to wake
I wish we were together now for goodness sake!

My Little Puppy Named Sue

It is warm and the sun is out,
the boy shouts

Lets go out side and play,
Mom says ok without delay

The puppy runs out,
he wanted to play too no doubt

The puppy jumps and plays,
licks and kisses that way

The boy laughs and giggles,
as the boy wiggles and wiggles

Mom begins to laugh and giggle too,
at this little puppy named Sue

I bet you would giggle too,
if you played with my little dog named Sue!

I Wait by the Fire Place

After a stressful day,
so much went on in so many ways
I come home and waited by the fireplace,
and lay on a pillow with trims of white lace
You came home and laid down next to me,
seeing how much I needed thee,
With such a tender hug,
as we lay snug as a bug
you hold me tight
you make everything seem alright
In your arms my soul felt claim inside
In your love my love abides
We watch the flickering of the firelight,
as the wood burns all night
We cuddle and share together,
and leave out side the cold winter weather
so nice snuggling with you
you love to snuggle with me too
as you hold me tight
I drift asleep and sleep all night
Knowing you keep me safe until morning light,
were I wake in front of the fireplace
You are not there not a trace
for you went to work for the day
Left me sleeping because you care that way
but I know after work you will come home to me,
because it is our home and our love we both need,
I smile and know you care
Thankful and grateful you were with me there,
knowing how much you love me laying on trims of white lace,
for you my love, I will wait by the fireplace!

We Share Our Memories

When we was in school I remember you,
When I was blue you remembered me too
For you made me laugh and smile back at you

When I had a problem you were there
Always showing me you care
Yes we were a pair

With our friendship so rare
No matter what, we were there
Picking up the pieces because we care

But now it is so hard for you,
My heart just brakes in two
For what I want to give to you

Is your health and happiness,
And plenty of good rest
So you can withstand the rest

Time that we shared
Proving time after time that we care,
And that we would always be there

So I just want to send to you this prayer,
God will always be with you there
And no matter what, you know God and I care

In my heart treasured friend
You'll always be there just how you have always been
Not just once, but time and time again

For in my heart dear friend we will never be apart
No matter whether we are near or far apart
You are my best friend deep in my heart!

Babe You Are My Valentine

You are my Valentine,
For now and until the end of time
I am so proud that you are mine
My sweet treasured Valentine
You are my Babe, my loving man
I love you with all that I am the best that I can
And because you loved me when you could of ran
That proves that you are a special man
You say it is just another day
Your right it is just another day
Another day that you have made me laugh and smile
Another day you have inspired me to travel another mile
Your sweetness and kindness is just you being you
You light up my world when I am blue
You work with me when I don't know what to do
You hold my hand and I know we will make it through
Because I love you and you love me too
Because I choose my life to share with you
because you have a caring spirit and I love that too
because you are always just you
So on this day that you say is just another day
I just wanted to take the time to say
I hope you have the most wonderful Valentine's Day!

Grants

I was searching for hope,
in ways that could help me to cope
So I went to learn of government grants and things,
I listened with all my being

But what I learned I was not prepared for,
within me I opened up more
My hopes just seemed to sore,
as the man talked and paced across the floor

They had grants for homes and jobs for you,
and many things for you to do
But I learned there is no government grants for love,
no grants to get you in the golden gates above

There are no grants to get respect,
no grants to protect
No grants that says they care,
no grants to assure they will be there

No grants to say you will not die,
no grants to find the answers to all the questions why
No grants to protect you from life's pain,
no grants protect you from life's rain

No grant to give a gift of Love,
no grant to let you walk with God above
They are just Government grants,
just grants with no feelings leaving you in a trains

They are just money grants for you,
no grants to tell you what to do
No grants to take away the blues,
no grants to warm you too

Just a forgiven Grant of Love,
a grant that God will always love you from above!

Do You Know?

Do you know how my heart bleeds for you?
Do you know how much I love you, too
Do you know how much I care?
Do you know that in the morning rush,
do you know I need your touch?
Do you know when you go to work and say good-bye,
do you know I need to see that love in your eye?
Do you know when I am sad,
do you know that it is you that makes me glad?
Do you know with every breath I give to you,
Do you know you take my breath away too?
Do you know when you make love to me,
do you know it is only you, with which my soul wants to be?
Do you know you make my spirit come alive with joy?
Do you know your a special lover not just a boy toy?
Do you know that with all that I am I care about you?
Do you know I love you too?
I just wish you knew!

Depression Pit

In the deepest pit of depression there is no light,
no sunshine, shining bright
To hate to see a smile
once treasured to have for a while
No one to understand
grinding against your soul like sand
Hiding your soul so they can not take
like the spirit that they break
Concerting your heart to the bottom of the pit,
hoping someday it all will quit
Hanging on to some part of hope,
struggling each day to cope
Feeling the person you were little by little leave,
the person you were you can not retrieve
Deepening the loneliness in your soul,
for which you have become so cold
A pit, a wall of stone around you,
can no one else see it too?
God what do I do?
When darkness steals your health and life from you,
I hate the pity people give you
because they don't know what to do
So they walk away and take with them my hope
because with me they simply can not cope
Depression, a black plauge of illness and decease eating at
your soul
Depression has now taken its tole
Doctors try to comfort with drugs like a blanket on a bed,
does not fix the problem mattress under the blanket,
can they not hear what I have said?
So much pain inside of me I cannot stand,

Why can they not understand?
deep depression pits in my soul,
Eat away my heart and spirit that use to be so bold
My talents dying and creativeness I no longer can do,
My heart aching and yearning for this to do
Depression pits started long ago,
Now face life or let life go
Depression,
ate away my hope of restoration,
I no longer have wisdom or whit,
only a life in a Depression Pit!

Don't Call Me a Family Friend

A friend that came to call,
He was short and not all tall
He wanted me to go swimming at a swimming hole
he was insistence and bold
but I told him no thank you, I had kids to baby set,
but if he wanted to he could set and talk a bit
I knew him for many years
My memories of him was clear,
He left and later came back,
I let him in and then he attacked,
we fought over the lamp,
Whiff, boom, and bamp
The kids woke up and came running
go get your grandpa I was summing
they ran
fast as they can
He tore at my clothes and pulled out a knife,
The moon reflected off that blade that night
he said he would kill me
I was shocked, why is this to be
This is wrong forcing me,
He is drunk and the knife blade I see,
My body, my clothes ripped,
I tried to pull away
My voice not a word I could say,
He looked for my children if he could see,
It scared the death out of me
The fear of him hurting them,
I thought, "My Dad will take care of them"

he took the blade that he had,
and shook it at me saying he would have me and he was mad,
Finally he left and ran,
What in God's name got into that man?
A scar in my life forever more,
As I stand looking at my clothes he had tore,
Covering up my bare scratched body I'm so ashamed,
Even though it is to him for this to blame,
and he feels no remorse or shame,
to him it was just a drunkerd's game!

Passionate You

Oh you are so passionate; yes that is true,
a candle you light and kiss me too
A warm smile comes over you,
You touch my lips with your fingertips,
Knowing it's your passion and love that I miss
The gown I wear you tenderly remove with care
It drops to the floor right there,
as you softly touch my hair
And show me how much you miss me and you care
Showing how grateful that I am there
With your finger it is my body you trace
that puts my heart running a fast race,
Hearing and breathing and your pleasure rings,
as our body connect with all things
Feeling the luring of your passionate touch
my soul becomes wet as the feeling rush
Sharing the feeling I love so much,
the spirit and soul dances and plays
In a joyous pleasure of ways,
together the touching and rushing of hands
You feel my body with all that you can,
the needing in your breathing I can hear
as you pull my body near
Your passion is so real and so dear,
you look at my naked body and you peer
As the deepening of your desires you begin to live
The adventure and exploring you give and give
I'm loving all that you do,
and I know you love it too
You thrust love inside of me all of you,
Yes…that passionate you!

Colors and All

As I set and paint with colors and tones,
The wind chills me in my bones
The sky is blue,
it looks so open too
I could just get lost looking at the sky,
asking all the questions and reasons why
Each cloud so different and yet the same,
some darken when it rains
Fall colors are the best,
The beautiful colors of flowers and the rest,
bright yellows and orange burgundy and browns
You can see them all through the towns
The seasons changes many times in life,
I am happy to share them with my wife
The birds with all their beauty I see,
I even see bright colors of the trees
God put color in all he sees,
making life beautiful both land and seas
He made big, short, and even tall,
all different in color each and all
God sees no different in us that is all,
for he loved us each one and all!

Drifting at an Ocean's Sea

Drifting away with me,
as the oceans drifts into the sea,
Drift, drifting away with me,
drifting in the ocean breeze
Drifting no one can see it be,
in moonlight pedals drifting in the ocean sea
What a beauty it is to be,
Rose pedals, moon light on the Ocean Sea
Drifting, drifting away with me,
the ocean reflects it up to see,
in moonlight rose pedals drifting away at sea

An Angel's Gift of a Rose

As a angel in a pure white dress,
Kneeled and placed a rose at rest,
without making a sound,
she gently placed it on the ground

She touched it with a kiss,
there she left it in the mist
Then with seemly nothing left to say,
the angel walked away

Her footprints did not leave a track,
nor did she ever look back
The rose was soon surrounded by a mist,
it seemed to swirl and twirl and twist

The rose had this sense of pleading,
a heart that was aching and bleeding
The angel knows what rose is seeking,
that is a secret the angel is keeping

On word and up word so went the mist,
giving the sight of a mystical twist
The rose now could hardly be seen,
but by sense that the rose was there was keen

Now clearing in the twirl of things,
a fling that almost sings
The leaves bending back,
in the swirling like sack

Then it became clear,
as I began to peer
Inside of the rose was so if to untwist,
inside the swirling mist

As the mist faded, the rose was in bloom,
a beauty that would consume
Even God's very own heart,
to see the elegance that is a part

Of this special rose's heart,
in which you now have become so much a part!

I Long for a Love Like You

My heart has only one beat to the rhythm,
it is a rhythm that beats only to your heart
A rhythm, which cannot be, torn apart,
a rhythm that is off the chart

My heart pumps with the rhythm of red blood,
each rhythm of the heart pumps out more love
Sealed with the twig of peace given by a dove,
showered by the blue skies up above

For if I had you,
no longer would I be blue
No longer would I search for you,
for I would have a love so true
For I long for a love just like you!

I Love You
Just as I Have Said

Passion is pure as a depth of red,
I think of you each night as I go to bed
I love you just as I have said,
but I wish I could hold you instead
As I dream of you in my head,
the heart is held together by a thread
As I hold on to each word that you have said,
my love for you is a passion of red,
I love you just as I have said!

What is Life About

Life with all it's truths and doubts,
not really sure what life is all about
As I sit and fish for some trout

Is life what we make it out to be,
or is life as simple as just what we see
Maybe life is about things we need it to be

Like the miles of Ocean Sea,
or the wide open skies as far as the eye can see
Or animals among the tall green trees,
or our family's love we see

Maybe life is about love in the air,
or friendships along being there
Maybe the problems that we bare

Maybe it is knowing God give all this in our care,
or just maybe, life is about knowing God is always there!

The Best of Holidays

It was a quiet night,
just looking at the Christmas lights
When I started to think,
how even the smallest of lights,
can bring so much delight
How even the tiniest smile,
stays in our memory for a long while
How each feeling of joy,
can be given with each little toy
As I decorate the tree,
I think what joy is found in friends that I see
Friends just like you and me
Blessed in all it's treasures you see
Have a Merry Christmas from me,
and a Happy New Year to thee!

God is Hearing You

I'm walking across the sandy dessert and it's hot,
each step I take burns my feet like red-hot fiery coals,
The load I'm carrying is so heavy,
I can hardly carry it
It makes each step I take burn even more as the weight from
my load pushes my feet into
the hot burning sand
I can feel my skin chapped from the hot dry winds that
pushes me back
But by the grace of God I moved just a little more down the
road of life,
I know God answers prayers,
So I asked God to please stop the wind
That it would make the road I have to travel easier if just the
wind would stop,
suddenly the wind did stop
The wind stopped so suddenly that I fell on my face
The hot burning sand burned into my chapped skin
My face felt as if it had jest been put into a fiery furnace,
I picked myself up and tried to dust the sand from my skin
I wondered why the Lord would let this happen to me
Wasn't I bearing enough pain already?
To dust the sand from my skin was like running sandpaper across it
Why? Kept running through my head
But then I wondered why he answered my prayer if he knew
it would only bring me more
pain in the long run?
Then a voice inside me said, "My child you asked me to stop
the wind,
that is what I did"
But you put no faith in me to know what was best,

you know that I would never ask you to carry a bigger load of
life than I knew you could
carry
You should have put your faith in me and ask me to relieve
you of some of your pain if it
be MY well,
to give you strength to bear and carry the heavy loads you
were called to carry"
Then my child you wouldn't have had to feel the burning sand
Your face and your chapped skin you wouldn't have to feel
the burning sand
Your face and your chapped skin wouldn't bleed from from
the sand being dusted off
I knew God was right and as I cried the salty tears run down my face
Each tear felt like alcohol on an open cut and the pain was great
The pain from the salty tears only brought more tears
But this pain didn't hurt as much as just knowing I was called
to bear it
Because I didn't have enough faith in the Lord Thy God
Where is your faith today?
Is it in God?

My Web of Words

In a big old Red barn, among a hay stack,
Watching a web for the spider to come back
Although it might not matter to some
to a chicken its dinner yummm
Each strand of web reaches out and touches
The spider's legs work and then hurries and rushes
it has a reason and a purpose for being there
Even though we don't notice and it's unaware,
of the purpose why they are there
Each strand matters and is important in our world,
as a spider web is, even in the wind that whirls
A web strand connects here and reaches to there,
like a bridge bonding to somewhere
Maybe I am but a spider in our world of things in part,
a spider that weaveth words that touches the heart
Some think my words to be just chatter,
maybe my words truly does mattered
It brought comfort to a soldier in a war,
it brought joy to a beggar that was poor
For I have touched a child of wonder,
made him stop and think and ponder
A soul searching to find its way when lost,
I gave a word of peace and direction, Hun you're not lost,
I have given comfort to a crying heart
Then went on our way because we had to part
I took a tear and replaced it with laughter
A treasured memory for here and ever after
My words touched the sick and give strength to heal
Now a life full of joy looks real
A heart of hate was replace with hope of love
now their life soars, as it should with grace from above,

I shared a sadden soul,
as life had taken its toll
I am but God's spider that weaveth a web strong as a rod
Reaching out with the grace of God
Because no matter where you live, or if you run
reach out and touch someone
The world is good and not all strife,
because we are the spider in this web of life!

Mary the Fairy

I know this fairy,
Her name is Mary
She is never contrary,
she's just happy to be Mary
She plays and never gets weary,
for she is just happy to be a fairy
We talked to our friend Larry,
and his friend Sarie
We all play games with Mary,
for she is a happy fairy
So give a big smile for Mary,
because she is a happy little fairy!

While You Are Away

While you are away,
I am at lose for words to say
I am so saddened and blue,
my heart flutters whenever I think of you
I can see your face in my mind,
that makes me impatient for the time
That you will return to me,
when you will then see
The longing I have for thee,
when I close my eyes and I can see you
In my arms I can feel you,
I can feel your embrace
But then I open my eyes and there is no trace,
of the man I love
If I could send to you my love,
my kisses and my hugs, by way of the dove
You are my life, my soul and my life long love!

Grateful to Be Together Through Time

The tenderness of your touch,
the feel of the breeze and the morning rush
The sweetness of your kiss,
all day I will miss
The start of a new day,
fresh in thought that way
The beauty of the flowers you gave to me,
brightened the smile that you see
You give me hope,
in each day that I must cope
We share life together,
through sunny and stormy weather,
We are a part,
of each other's heart
Two eyes that are not blind
but loving and kind
Our spirits are in time,
Together like rhythm and rhyme
Treasured and cherished through out our time,
so greatful for your life and mine

A Quiet Good Bye

As I set waiting and I sigh
Here in this air-o-plane so high
I drink my pop and eat my chips,
then carefully I blot my lips
I watch the clouds passing by,
I wonder how we fly so high
A quiet moment as time goes by,
I listen to the engines as we fly
I set and can't help but cry,
in death to my friend I had to say good-bye

This Little Angel

I have made for you this little angel with my own two hands
Just as God had planned,
a talent, a gift God have to me,
for all the world to see
While it can not take away your sad or disappointing times
Nor your hard and painful times
It is a gentle reminder of what God has planed,
just as he planned the skies and ocean sand
For God in His master piece that he has skillfully designed
just right
Is…The Grand Performance of Life
He has hand picked with great love and taught,
and a great deal of confidence in all the acts he has brought
For he has hand picked you to play,
his grand staring role in this way
For you life our your life just as he has planned,
working, appreciating and loving all you can
With every sadness and every joy,
with each girl and boy
To share your life and love,
just as he does from above
All though you can't always see the joy or it's summing,
just wait for God, he has it planned for you and it is a coming,
For you are,
his bright and shining stars!

You Are What Lights Up My Life

You are more than the sum of worlds,
you are more than the sum of love
You are more than the sum of sex,
you are more than the sum of money
You are more than the sum of things gained
You are more than the sum, of which I am
You are more than the sum of my works
and deeds,
for you God are the sum of all things,
you are the sum of what lights up my life!

Oh My Dear Mom

Oh my dear Mom,
let me tell you this
For all the times I didn't listen,
for all the times I made wrong choices
For all the times I wanted to tell you,
I love you every day
For all the times I could have but didn't
I want to say this to you Mom,
I love you
I lerned more than you think,
like faith and be faithful
For I knew God was with me always,
I knew you would always love me
Even though you didn't love my choices,
I know how much you are hurting
Without me on earth with you,
but Mom, I want to tell you this
God is faithful for he gave me you,
to share with me for a while
But now I choose to be your angel,
for when times are hard, God carries you,
and I will walk beside you
I will sing you my song of love,
you will not have to worry
For God promises to be there for you,
I must go and be your angel
But just remember this Mom,
God and I are only a prayer away
When ever you think of me,
I will be right here with you
Mom let me tell you this,

I choose faith and love
I am proud as I can be,
for God chose you for my mom
I choose to be your angel,
now I can be with you always
Ever minute of every day,
do not worry of things that are to come
For God has a plan,
I want to tell you how proud I am
For your strength and your faith,
for your time and your understanding
God made a perfect choice,
when he chose you as my Mom!
Signed your,
Angel

My Quiet Moment,
A Blessing to Me

I got up this morning and watched the squirrel,
It was hiding nuts in the green grass for winter
I listened to the birds singing
The wild geese was flying over head,
I watched the leaves falling
from the colorful trees
I felt the coolness in the air
I feel the fall is here
I rock the baby asleep
Life goes by so fast yet
I look at the simple things,
and life seems so slow for just a moment
I stop and think of my many blessings
My family, friends and loved ones
and I stop and think of all the little ones
that has no family or friends
my heart bleeds in pain for them
I feel helpless to help them,
my heart is heavy
I sing Amazing grace,
and I cry!

My Precious Mother

My mother took a seed within her,
she grew a precious child
My mother teaches and protects me,
that always meant alot to me
She shares my good times,
she also bares my hard and sad times
She always gives me a smile,
she comforts me across the miles
But the gift she gave just for me,
is her never-ending love that I will always see
And I love her, and that will always be!

Happy Mothers Day!

On This Night

I think of you all day,
why do I think that way?
Why do I linger on what you say?

I miss you all day and all night,
and dream of you and that is all right
but yet I still long for you to hold me tight

If I cannot hear your words today,
it makes my stomach sick that way
I miss you wanting me to stay

Let me tell you this,
for it is my wish
and is sealed with my kiss

If I shall die tonight,
it would be all right,
for my arms has held you tight

So if I die this night,
I will have loved you in the moonlight,
I have loved you in the sun's delight

If I shall die tonight,
I will die happy this night
because I have loved you with all of my might!

When I Feel You

I see in your eyes a feeling that burst,
into a beautiful smile
Embraced in the sharing,
a look of sincere caring
When I feel your kisses upon my lips,
I experience the warmth of butterflies
With the touch of your chest,
I feel the depth of love in your heart
When I feel your arms around me,
I feel the hope of a new day
I feel you take my cares away,
you give my mornings bright light
You fill my days with happiness and delight,
when you are not next to me,
I feel your spirit within me
The world I feel like I hold
When I feel your love so strong and bold,
but I can feel your soul,
It is then,
that I feel you have made, my life whole!

A Day of Wonder

In a stream of water I see,
a reflection of me
I drop a pebble and what do I see?
Ring after ring of ripples I see
As I look to the depth of the water,
I wonder why do I bother
I feel the water in my hand,
I see the bottom and there is sand,
Still I wonder,
about of my life I do ponder
So I take a walk,
to the trees and leaves I do talk
With no sound of their reply,
I get up and leave and say good-bye!

Mommy and Daddy's Baby

I was in Heaven, just waiting to see,
just whose baby I'd be
I was picked and that tickled me,
to think of them looking at me
God picked them especially for me,
they are loving and kind,
and they are mine
Each with a warm smile,
to sleep I'll go
As mommy touches my toe,
they lay me down to sleep
I lay there and not a peep,
I dream and I see,
Just how happy I am to be
My Mommy and Daddy's little baby

Did You Know Son?

I gave you life before I gave you birth,
for you filled my life with worth
Did you know son?
You filled my heart with the warmth of an evening sun,
I watched you when you went from a walking to a run
Did you know Son?
I watched you grow from playing in sand,
into a caring and loving gentleman
Did you know Son?
I watched you in the ups and downs of life,
now I watch you take your Wife
Did you know Son?
I was never more proud of you,
than the day you said Mom I love you too!
Did you know Son?
Did you know just how much I love you?
Or how blessed I feel in seeing what you do,
Did you know Son?
On this day Mom still loves you tons and tons!

I'm a Baby to Be

I can hear and feel the vibrations of my mommy's singing
just before the telephone starts it's ringing

I can feel my Daddy's hands there to protect me,
bet he wonders what I will grow up to be

I am not here alone,
I hear my brother's heart tones

Yes you guessed it, we are twins,
one day we will be full of giggles and grins

Two sets of grandparents you see,
that means twice as much to spoil me

It is so warm and comforting here within,
Mommy rubs her tummy time and time again

I bet my Daddy is a handsome man,
for he reaches for me with a gentle hand

I will keep growing and be healthy in every way,
and soon I will come out to stay

And then I will say,
Hurray, two babies today

Hello world I am here, it's my birthday!

My Amazing Grace

When I look into the heavens,
I see God's Amazing Grace

When I see so many blessings around me,
then I see My amazing grace

I see the flower and the trees,
amazing grace it much be

When I give birth to a child,
blessings and faith in this Amazing Grace

I see the power in a touch that taketh away a tear,
I felt the power of My Amazing Grace

My smiles are touching and healing,
so I share My Amazing Grace

You gave a rib of your side and beside you I will stay,
because we share An Amazing Grace

When you touched my face with such tenderness,
I consume your kindness and your Amazing Grace

I found An Amazing Grace in you,
I shared your friendship and your love too

as I sang to God in praise,
for My Amazing Grace!

A Beloved Mother's Love

A beloved Mother's love is shared,
and her life she prepared

For all the things that was to come,
many good times, bad times yes there were some

You could see her love reflected,
in her children's love that she protected

Grandchildren, what laughter and what fun,
oh the joy she had when she watched them was tons,

Friends she shared with and enjoyed,
and to life she gave and employed

All the love she could,
she worked harder than she should

But her heart and love she gave to you,
because she knew you loved her too

Because that is what a beloved Mother is to do,
even though she is gone she still loves you!

In a Room of Rhymes

Once upon a time,
in a room made of rhymes

A child sits and reads,
of a garden full of works and deeds

The child giggles and laughs,
as she passes a little gas

She reads of blue skies,
and of kite ties way up in the skies

She asks so many questions of why,
then she sits and sighs

She just looks and does not read,
as her eyes closes to a little bead

She falls peacefully asleep,
she does not make a peep

Fast asleep,
in Gods hands she sleeps!

A Mother's Passing Love

When you were born life just begun,
I was proud you were my son
As you grew older,
you became a bit bolder
But I was still proud as I could be,
that we shared life you and me
But when it was time for you to leave,
I sent you my love but I was still proud as I could be
You grew up to be a fine young man,
doing in life the best that you can
But now it is time for me to go,
Son always remember, I love you so
But Son it is time for passing for me,
so remember here deep in my heart you see
Son I'm still as proud as I can be,
that we shared life together you and me!

The War and Me

We go to war and we fight for our right,
so we can hold our loved ones tight
To be treated like a human being,
to be treated fairly as we are human beings,
but some how when I am covered with dirt,
every thread is wet from sweat on my shirt
and guns are shooting and mines all around,
and I look down the barrow of my gun,
I see what we call the enemy that runs,
where it is kill or be killed
It puts you to the test of your will,
where I know that those I fight
also fight for what they think is right,
Soldiers are we, so we fight again,
I am with my gun in hand
Fighting for our family's freedom the best I can,
I hear the guns blasting and I see the faces
Bodies that lies each shot and wasted
I cry silent tears inside for this night,
to make my life come out right
For it is kill or be killed
I must be strong willed
In a flash a thought of my mother,
as she sews a hand made cover,
for my bed, God knows I love her,
My loved ones I am missing
an end to this war I am wishing
the gun goes off and I kill a man,
oh Lord help me if you can
I must stand and fight and be a soldier and a man,
sick at my stomach I took his life,

at the end of his gun was taped a knife,
Silent tears I cry inside
Then flashes again came of momma in my head,
colors blue, green and red,
for me is what she said,
A beautiful cover for my bed
I love you son echoes in my head,
Guns again I hear so near
I look out and there I peer
A gun pointed right at me,
Kill or be killed
God is with me,
Scared to death I closed my eyes and see,
angel surrounding me,
God Help me is my plea

God please save me,
My gun shoots and their he lies,
with open eyes,
I say a prayer for him,
I hate we have no time to burry them
We push on and I cry inside,
In God's love I hide
and in his mercy I reside,
in the law of the land I must abide
Even if it kills me inside
The day is gone and I must rest,
for another day put to the test
I close my eyes to rest,
in my mind my memory they are the best,
I thank God for all the rest
Even when life puts me to a test,
I know God made Solider his very best!

I Caught a Falling Angel

She said I caught a falling angel,
caught her in the arms of my song
She said she needed to be strong,
she had cried way to long
Although I didn't know her,
she said I caught a falling angel,
caught her in the arms of my song
I didn't know angels needs were so strong,
I didn't even know they heard my songs
With tears in my eyes, I couldn't see
She begun to say these words to me
I spread my wings, let angels sing,
throughout heaven let their voices ring
With blessed thanks to you I bring,
Sing them loud and sing them strong
The best of songs to you now belong,
for you caught this falling angel with a song
So lift up your voice,
Let us rejoice,
Heaven rings and angels sings,
you have blessed us with your songs that you sing

In Honor of My Mother and Memory of My Dad

Dad I wish you were here to sing one of your silly songs,
you know the ones you made up when things went wrong
I miss the little poems that showed you understood,
I try to respect you the best I could
and Mamma too, the best I can
I'll never forget my Daddy's Hands
My life was the hardest it had ever been
I set down and thought of you and then,
I thought, what would you have done back then?
You would have made up a silly songs of it to sing to me
Just to match me grin, then a smile you'd see,
then you'd laugh and start to sing another song
Then the problems seemed to melt away before long
Or you'd write a poem of how it seemed to you
In that frankness, I'd find an answer of what to do
You'd be proud, I still write poetry by the way,
they read my Poetry in Washington in DC today,
it was to honor my achievements in poetry you see,
so I am as proud as I can be
But the honor is because of the gift you gave to me,
and in Honor of Mom who loves and shares it with me
So Dad, I just wanted you to see
these awards and honors that I receive
is really meant for my folks that has helped me be,
all, that god has meant for me to be
For you both loved us all it was plain to see,
so, in honor of my Mother and memory of my Dad,
and all the love to us you both made sure we had!
I write this poem to you,

I am so greatful for all you both took time to do, and because Dad you know I still love you!

Mother's Wisdom

Mother had always said to me,
"Paper won't refuse ink"
I didn't understand back then,
but as time in my life went on,
I grew to know Mom's wisdom
Her teachings to be carried on,
now it is my turn to pass along
To my children my wisdom,
in life I have learned
Many things of wisdom along the way,
so I add to my Mother's wisdom
These things to my children I say,
"Paper won't refuse ink,
but eyes will refuse to see,
what the ears refuse to hear"
These learnings and memories,
I have come to treasure
Within the face of the truths of,
My Mother's Wisdom!

My Letter from Momma

Son, I was thinking of you, so I came here to the park,
the sun is shining and the breeze is blowing
Peaceful and calm the river looks so inviting,
Son, because we have lost loved ones in the war,
and you being in the service, in my mind I have fear
And in my eye is a mother's loving tear,
but here in my heart, I'm proud as I can be,
So son you see,
I see your laughter and I can see your smiles
Son you know our children is our hearts and souls
In my heart and mind are treasures to behold,
My precious memories of you so vivid and bold,
Son, my missing you is growing stronger each day
By the way, I got word they published my poem today,
I'm bursting with pride I must say
When you need your momma to tell you, It'll be ok,
you can click on poetry.com I'm there any day,
But Son know that in my heart, I love you every day
as I started to fold up my letter from momma,
my tears streaming from my eye and my heart heavy,
I looked up and thought I seen angels
with wings on high as they fly through the sky,
I thought surely not
I visualized my momma singing
and times she would tell me its ok, and to be strong
I looked down at my hands and thought to myself,
how proud of momma I am
She grabbed the opportunity to share with the world,
all that she shares with me every day
Her poetry yes, but more than that
God bless my momma,

now she shares with the world her love too
So grateful for my memories and my letter,
I grab the letter and held it to my heart and cried
I love you too momma,
I looked up so grateful,
for my love and my letter, from my Momma!

In My Garden of Life

Just like my vegetable garden, I grow
weeds pop up here and there and everywhere you go,
some go unnoticed, which becomes a problem for me,
smothering out the beauty of the garden that we see
Sometimes even causing vegetables to wither and die
So I must pull and pluck out weeds or at least try
to insure the beauty and the fruit of the garden is there
for all to look, enjoy, eat and share because I care,
My garden of life is like my vegetable garden you see
the beauty is there for us to share just all it's meant to be
I have to remove the weeds to share what is inside of me
to show what their time and caring has meant to me
In my garden of life there are many that care
My folks, family and best friends they are always there
but others also show how much they care
Some lend a hand, a smile, or just by being there
Some a poem, a song, or a calming prayer
some with finances, work, teaching and giving
some support what I do, even in loving and living
This is all in My Garden of Life too
so in my appreciation for all you do,
I clear the weeds from my garden so it can be seen
That it is all of us together that has made up this scene
I stand here today so tall and proud,
in front of this amazing crowd,
to show the beauty of the fruits of their labors and seeds
will live on through me in the works and deeds,
for I could not have gotten here today, I must say
if each of you had not been beside me all the way
for you are a part of what makes up my life
Here in My Garden of Life!